CAMPING HEALTHY
Hygiene for the Outdoors

by
Buck Tilton, M. S.
&
Rick Bennett, Ph.D.

Illustrations
by
Marc Bohne

I C S BOOKS
Merrillville, Indiana

Camping Healthy, *Hygiene for the Outdoors*

ICS Books, Inc.
1370 East 86th Place
Merrillville, Indiana 46410
800-541-7323

Printed in the U.S.A.
All ICS titles are printed on 50% recycled paper from pre-consumer waste. All sheets are processed without using acid.

Library of Congress Cataloging-in Publication Data

Tilton, Buck.
     Camping Healthy:Hygiene for the Outdoors / by Buck Tilton, M.S. & Rick
Bennett, Ph.D.
        p. cm.
     Includes index & bibliographical references
     ISBN 1-57034-010-2
     1. Camping—Health aspects.   I. Bennet, Rick, Ph. D.   II. Title.
RC1220.M6T549   1995
   613.6'7—dc20   95-2550
                                         CIP

Contents

Water Disinfection: Chapter Eight, 34

Keeping A Klean Kitchen: Chapter Nine, 45

The Healthy Zoo: Chapter Ten, 48

Appendix A: Sanitizers & How They Work, 58

Appendix B: Resources, 63

Index, 65

Dedication

For all the great practitioners of applied microbiology who have ventured into the wilderness of ignorance and poverty to apply their knowledge in order to lessen the suffering caused by food- and water-borne disease.

And for my dad and mom, Jim and Eris Tilton, who still hope someday I'll clean up my act.

Introduction: *Chapter One*

In the Beginning, or shortly after, millions of years before you arrived, they were here. When you are gone, when we are all gone, they will probably still be here. Everywhere you go, they go too. Everywhere you stop, some of them are already waiting. They are a part of you and a part of everything you do. From the stream to the latrine, from the nose to the mouth, from the blister to the boil, from the water bottle to the lump of leftover macaroni, they are involved. Germs!

Cleanliness might be next to godliness but improper hygiene and the resulting transmission of germs may put you even closer, having sent more people on to the afterlife than all other reasons to die combined. Before hygiene there was the Bubonic Plague, the Curse of Cholera, and Typhoid Mary. Caused by the bacteria Yersinia pestis, the "Black Death" alone, in a three year period (1347 to 1350), wiped out an estimated 25 million Europeans and laid approximately nine-tenths of the population of England underground.

Those days of un-hygienic mass migrations to the hereafter are over … perhaps. Humanity has had the audacity to think many microbes were "under control," but everyone who can read knows old enemies are returning (e.g., cholera, malaria resistant to anti-malarial drugs, tuberculosis resistant to antibiotics, virulent strains of streptococcus-A dubbed the "flesh-eating bacteria") and new scourges are on the rise (e.g., AIDS).

As an outdoorsperson you might think the great majority of germs (a scientific term representing all the microscopic things that might infect a human and cause disease) lurk in the wilderness waiting for a suitable host to pass near enough for an attack. Not so. In fact, in most cases, the contrary is true: the germs hitched a free ride into the wilderness with you or some other unwary bipedal primate. As more and more Homo sapiens show up more and more often in backcountry areas, the presence of humans, even if only for a short while, builds a community of disease possibilities.

Check out this compilation of data from the World Health Organization (WHO). These are the major sources of concern:

Infectious Disease	Cause	Annual Human Deaths
Pneumonia	Bacteria or Virus	4,300,000
Diarrheal Illness	Bacteria or Virus	3,200,000
Tuberculosis	Bacteria	3,000,000
Hepatitis B	Virus	1,500,000
Malaria	Protozoa	1,000,000
Measles	Virus	880,000
Tetanus	Bacteria	600,000
AIDS	Virus	550,000
Whooping Cough	Bacteria	360,000

Source: WHO, Harvard School of Public Health, 1990.

The list above should give you a very important message. Although wilderness visitors are placing more and more emphasis on concerns like the water-borne protozoan Giardia lamblia, they downplay their contact with other humans and other sources of disease in the outdoor environment. While it sure enough is important to plan for effective water disinfection (see Chapter Eight), very few humans will be hospitalized and even fewer will die of giardiasis.

Of the above list of who's-who in killers of humanity, only two may be considered "environmental": (1) Tetanus is a disease caused by a bacteria, Clostridium tetani, found in soil. It can be eliminated as a risk to backcountry adventurers by the safe and effective tetanus vaccine. (2) Malaria, a disease found almost exclusively in tropical regions, is caused by four species of protozoa of the genus Plasmodia, carried in the wild and transmitted by bloodthirsty mosquitoes. Most malarial diseases can be prevented by the ingestion of anti-malarial drugs prior to exposure to the protozoa.

The rest of the diseases on the list above, and many more, are carried by humans and passed to other humans. Your safety in relation to disease is primarily a matter of "common sense" and prevention. The fact that you travel into regions where men and women are as rare as four-leafed clovers is no reason for a false sense of security. With wilderness increasingly trammeled by Leave-A-Trace individuals and groups, there now exists ample justification for being careful. "Wilderness Injuries and Illnesses," an article in the July 1992 Annals of Emergency Medicine, reports: "The injury and illness patterns indicate that wilderness medical efforts should concentrate on wilderness hygiene..." In a wild setting, without the "conveniences" of hot water, flushing toilets and options to safely discard wastes, greater thought and care are needed to keep the germs—your germs—from getting into other humans and the environment.

The goal of this book is to provide some science tempered with common sense in order to make your wilderness trip as safe from germs as possible.

The Life & Times of Germs:
Chapter Two

Not all germs are bad and many microbes, in fact, are essential for your life and the health of the living world. But some are indeed really bad guys, extracting a huge toll in cost, suffering and death. The nasties, however, excepting disease agents such as HIV (the AIDS virus) and plague bacteria, do not have the ability to infect and cause disease in every human they happen to encounter. When disease results it is the visible, and certainly felt, expression of a battle being waged between the microbe and the less-than-fortunate host. In the battle of the germs you may be the "host." To your involuntary credit and your ability to survive, there are many tricks up your evolutionary sleeve. Although you are called a host, your body goes to great effort not to be one. This attribute is called "disease resistance" and can be further explained as a set of non-specific and specific factors.

As a non-specific example, your skin is a marvelous barrier to the microbial world. Witness what happens when human skin is burned to the second or third degree: infection almost always occurs. Healthy skin also has its own microbial army that digests skin oil and produces a protective acid barrier that inhibits invaders such as

Staphylococcus aureus, a bacteria abundantly present on skin and in the noses of many humans.

Specific resistance arises from your immune system as it produces protein antibodies and from special blood cells called lymphocytes. These antibodies and special cells can seek out and inactivate a variety of microbial intruders.

The point here is simple: not all exposure to disease agents results in disease. The right number of invaders has to be in the right place at the right time in the right host. You can take advantage of the situation by doing common and simple things to swing the balance and turn the tide of war in your favor. This basic understanding of parasite-host interaction can provide the basis for sound sanitation decisions in the backcountry. Your task is to implement prevention into the day-to-day experiences of life outdoors. Read on.

The Evil-Doers

The "bugs" of most concern are called "pathogens": germs that cause at least some "pathos" (suffering) as part of their nature. Some pathogens are more pathological than others, and some hosts are more susceptible. Hence the degree of pathos is a product of the attributes of the bug and the host. Some humans, you will have noticed, tend to be continuously ill while others seem to be superhumanly immune.

Microbiologists, members of an odd and often morbid lot, class microbes by their biological complexity. In order of increasing complexity, the microbes are called either virus, bacteria, fungi and yeast, protozoa or the larger parasites. The microbes that are clear-cut pathogens have some unique biological characteristics that create chinks in their armor that you can exploit to save your "skin." These "chinks" are mentioned briefly below with each evil-doer.

VIRUSES

Some viruses can survive for long periods outside of living tissue, yet they require a living cell that they can enter and redirect in order to replicate new virus particles. They are unimaginably tiny, and account for the respiratory infections that are responsible for approximately one-half of all acute illnesses. Major viruses include influenza, the common cold, mumps and measles. Some viruses set up housekeeping in the central nervous system and cause forms of meningitis and encephalitis. Herpes simplex virus type-1 causes cold sores and herpes simplex virus type-2 causes genital lesions. The Epstein-Barr virus produces infectious mononucleosis. Varicella-zoster causes chicken pox that may later appear as shingles. Viruses cause hepatitis and AIDS.

Two viruses cause approximately 88 percent of all food and water-related viral illnesses.

1. Norwalk virus, named for Norwalk, Ohio, where it was first isolated, makes more people sick than any other food-related virus. It's passed easily from one sufferer to another by hand and mouth, and rolls into high gear 24 to 48 hours after contact has been made. Though it lasts about a week, the problems of vomiting and diarrhea are relatively mild, rarely requiring a doctor's care.

2. Hepatitis A can be swallowed with some fecal-contaminated foods and water. Undercooked shellfish from water polluted with human wastes has been a common source of hep A. It can spread through sharing water bottles and utensils, improperly washing hands (an example of the fecal-oral route) and intimate contact between people. Stomach pain, nausea, vomiting, fatigue and loss of appetite show up 15 to 50 days after ingestion. Severe cases may cause jaundice (yellowing of the skin and whites of the eyes) and dark urine. Hepatitis B produces similar but more severe symptoms, but it's transmitted primarily by blood contact.

HIV: A CASE IN POINT

AIDS stands for Acquired Immune Deficiency Syndrome, a sincerely life-threatening infection that destroys the body's ability to fight off other types of infections. AIDS is the final, completely fatal stage of a continuum of problems caused by the Human Immunodeficiency Virus (HIV). Once the HIV is in human blood, antibodies to the virus develop which will show up in a blood test. Seropositivity (testing positive for a certain antibody) usually shows up four to six weeks after HIV infection. It is communicated by blood-and-body fluid transmission. Saliva, tears, sweat, urine, semen, vaginal secretions and stool can all carry the HIV, but only blood and semen have been known to transmit the virus.

Patients who have been infected but have not yet developed the antibodies are considered to be in the first stage of the continuum. Stage two patients have the antibodies but no symptoms of the disease. Once signs and symptoms appear, the patient may still not be technically classified as an AIDS sufferer. For a while, this stage was called the AIDS-related complex (ARC).

But regardless of the stage of the disease, the HIV-infected patient can pass the virus.

Chinks in Viral Armor: Although antibiotics are generally of no value in treating viruses, most of them are inactivated by heat, ultraviolet light and some sanitizers.

BACTERIA

There are thousands of different species and strains of bacteria. Most of these plant-like critters perform essential ecological functions such as the decay of fallen trees and the conversion of rotting animal tissue to release nitrogen for plant nutrition: parts of the Grand Scheme. Being like small invisible plant cells, bacteria can grow and reproduce free in the environment. Their life cycle is not dependent on a source of living mammalian cells as are viruses.

Bacteria have a distinct cell wall, much the same as plants, but must absorb their food from the environment instead of converting carbon dioxide and water into sugar as plants are able to do. It is the cell wall that gives bacteria some of their toughness and resistance to drying and chemicals. Bacteria, like some insects, have developed unique adaptations to the poisons in their world, making many of the common antibiotics useless today.

Bacteria are classified fundamentally by a procedure that prepares them for viewing under a microscope. Bacteria will stain either red or blue in the Gram reaction (a method of staining bacteria developed by Hans Gram, a Danish physician). Red-staining bugs are Gram negative, and blue-staining bugs are Gram positive.

Bacteria are further grouped by their shape which is either (1) a coccus (the plural is cocci), a spheroid or oval or ball-shape, and (2) a rod-shape that ranges from very long thin rods to short stubby rods that often appear as cocci (making the work of the microbiologist tricky from time to time).

Members of the Gram positive cocci include Staphylococcus aureus (a.k.a. Staph) and Streptococcus (a.k.a. Strep). "Streptococci" means chain-forming cocci which appear under the microscope as a chain of oh-so-unpleasant pearls.

Staph. aureus lives on the skin and in the noses of at least one-half of all humans and typically causes little harm until it finds a foothold in the host's resistance. Ugly conditions such as boils, abscesses, wound infections and pneumonia often find Staph involved. If conditions are right this pest will grow rapidly on things like tuna salad and dairy products. A tuna sandwich carried in a lunchbag in a backpack on a warm day for a few hours can send you rushing behind bushes for six to eight hours with nausea and vomiting.

The Streptococci are seldom associated with food- and water-borne illnesses. They are usually shared one person to another. The Strep diseases are notorious: (1) Scarlet fever took a tremendous toll before the days of milk pasteurization. (2) Rheumatic fever, even today, damages the valves of the heart in seriously diseased children. (3) Strep pneumonia is often the real cause of death among humans with serious long-term disease problems of another source.

Many other Gram positive bacteria live in soil (e.g., Clostridium tetani) and water (e.g., Bacillus ceres, a source of mild diarrhea in humans, and Bacillus anthrasis, the anthrax agent).

Some of the Gram negative bacteria such as Haemophilus influenzae (bacterial flu), Neisseria meningititis (meningitis), and Bordetella pertussis (whooping cough) cause severe and life-threatening infections of the airway and brain. There is virtually no risk of developing these diseases in the backcountry unless you were exposed before your trip.

Some of the Gram negative bacteria, on the other unclean hand, often travel with you in your food and your bowels. Fecal matter from animals, wild and domestic, also packs a few unpleasant punches. All feces are loaded with Gram negative bacteria. Human stool contains an average 100 billion (100,000,000,000) bacteria per gram—almost one-third of the fecal mass. The most common potential pathogen in poop is Escherichia coli (see below).

The role of bacteria in food-borne disease is common headline news. In the United States, six bacteria are blamed for over 90 percent of all dietary-related bacterial illnesses.

1. Bacillus cereus lives as a spore, a dry seed-like structure in grains and spices, and germinates when the food is moist and when contaminated cooked food is improperly stored. Stomach pain, nausea and vomiting, sometimes mild diarrhea, usually occur within eight to 16 hours of ingestion. The problem almost always self-limits in less than 24 hours.

2. Staphylococcus aureus (see above) may drop off of contaminated hands into breakfast, lunch and dinner. S. aureus multiplies with great speed in protein-rich foods at warm temperatures. Rather than an infectious disease, the bacteria produce a toxin. The reaction that erupts suddenly 30 minutes to six hours after you've eaten produces cramps, vomiting, diarrhea, headache, sweats and chills. Although the problem may last one to two days, medical treatment is seldom required unless you let yourself get seriously dehydrated.

3. Shigella most often gets into you from food and water contaminated with fecal matter, usually from the hands of he or she who last handled the food and water. Shigellosis causes dysentery bloody, mucus-ridden diarrhea), fever, bad stomach cramps, and a search for a doctor. Illness will probably appear less than four days after ingestion, but some cases have shown up seven days later.

4. Salmonella are common in eggs and occasionally in dairy products. Within an average of 12 to 24 hours, sometimes faster, symptoms appear: stomach pain, diarrhea, nausea, vomiting, headache, chills, weakness, thirst. Fever may be present. Although cases have

been known to become severe, most people recover by drinking lots of fluids and waiting in distress.

5. Campylobacter jejuni contaminates meats primarily, especially chicken, although some types are common in backcountry water and fecal matter. The likelihood of contacting the bacteria increases if you handle raw or eat undercooked flesh. An average of four to seven days passes after ingestion before you get stomach pain and bloody diarrhea. The problem may last two to seven days. Find a doctor.

6. Clostridium perfringens is found in meat usually stored at too warm a temperature before serving. Eight to 22 hours later abdominal cramps, nausea and diarrhea may make you think it's all over. Vomiting, headache, fever and chills are rare with C. perfringens. Symptoms usually go away harmlessly within 36 hours.

Other bacteria deserving Honorable Mention as possible food-borne pathogens include: Vibrio, Brucella and Yersinia enterocolitica. They cause, in general, diarrhea, nausea and/or vomiting. Less honorable and less common, several food-borne bacteria have been known to cause death in the U. S. in recent years: Listeria monocytogenes, Salmonella typhimurium and Clostridium botulinum. Storing food too warm, dirty food handlers and improper processing have been the cause of outbreaks.

E. COLI: A CASE IN POINT

No one's stool smear will ever win Garden Beautiful, but every human intestinal tract flowers with a variety of bacteria living in a healthy symbiotic relationship with the involuntary gardener. Normal gut flora for an average person weighs in at three to four pounds, and includes Clostridium, Streptococcus and numerous strains of Escherichia coli. Most E. coli are strains that have little ability to produce disease, but some strains with great pathos have been incriminated in serious disease outbreaks. As many as 92 percent of the seriously ill patients, where the source could be traced, got sick from food stored at improper temperatures and poor personal hygiene of food handlers.

Like most bacterial pathogens, E. coli cannot be frozen to death and will multiply slowly even at temperatures as low as 44°F, but it can be killed by thorough cooking. A major source of "traveler's diarrhea," E. coli survives well in water contaminated with feces. E. coli may be found in a bladder infection, septic shock from wound infections and a ruptured appendix.

Chinks in Bacterial Armor: Some antibiotics are effective in the treatment of bacterial infections. Most are killed by sanitizers, high temperatures and ultraviolet light.

FUNGI AND YEAST

Fungi are primitive plant-like lifeforms that tend to favor moist environments and feed on living plants, decaying organic matter … and animal tissue. Fungal infections are usually bothersome but relatively mild in terms of disease processes. Athlete's foot, for instance, is caused by one of several dermatophytes (fungal parasites that grow on skin): Tricophyton rubrum, Tricophyton mentagrophytes, Epidermophyton floccosum. Ringworm and vaginal yeast infections are included in the list of fungal infections. Fungi generally produce itching, pain and scaling. In the immunosuppressed a fungal infection called candidiasis can be overwhelming and fatal.

Chinks in Fungal Armor: Common antibiotics are of little value and fungi can be resistant to sanitizers, but special fungicidal liquids, ointments and powders usually work. Keeping your skin clean and dry helps defeat fungal infections. Exposure to ultraviolet light may be helpful.

PROTOZOA

Protozoa are a phylum of the animal kingdom that includes the most simple creatures, most of them unicellular.

Giardia lamblia parasites swim or float around as cysts in many wilderness water sources and spread through fecal contamination by humans and other animals. Giardiasis ranks as the most common water-borne illness in the United States. Unpleasant, but typically benign, the illness usually causes more than a week of diarrhea with bloating, flatulence and stomach cramps. Symptoms take about 10 days to show up, but the parasites may hang around inside for weeks before you feel sick. Some patients never develop the typical signs and symptoms of giardiasis. They have periodic mild cramping and bloating, but they never explode with diarrhea. Some carriers of Giardia lamblia are asymptomatic.

Cryptosporidium protozoa, although transmittable via food and body contact, are primarily water-borne parasites. They get in the water from feces of infected animals, including humans. Explosive diarrhea and tummy cramps appear after an incubation period of four to 14 days, and self-limit, going away after five to 11 miserable days.

Parasitic protozoa include the four species of Plasmodia that cause malaria.

Chinks in Protozoal Armor: Heating water to the boiling point, most filters, and properly used chemical disinfectants will rid water of viable Giardia lamblia. Cryptosporidium are thick-walled and resistant to chemical disinfectant, but they can be filtered out by the same filters that remove Giardia, or cooked to death in water that reaches boiling (see Chapter Eight).

PREVENTION: TAKING THE CRAMPS OUT OF CAMP

Prevention of environmental diseases relies on awareness and practical methods (e.g., tetanus vaccinations, water disinfection). The obvious bottom line in the prevention of communicable diseases is universal body-substance precautions with all humans. It is safest to disregard thoughts of "this is a high risk person" and "this is a low risk person." Consider all people as potential transmitters of infectious disease. Prevention requires, more than anything else, a change in behavior. Keep in mind that the community of diseases, especially in the wilderness, are sometimes passed around a group by very casual means.

1. Contact with blood poses the greatest risk, and disposable rubber gloves should be carried in wilderness first aid kits... and worn! Or, if the wound is minor, direct the patient in the cleaning of their own wound.

2. Double-bag in plastic all soiled bandages and dressings if they cannot be completely burned in an environmentally safe, hot fire.

3. Use a pocket mask with a one-way valve when performing mouth-to-mouth breathing.

4. Wash your hands before and after treating a sick or injured person (see Chapter Three).

5. Do not share bandannas, toothbrushes, razors, water bottles, eating utensils, etc.

6. Wash and dry all community kitchen gear and keep anyone remotely suggestive of illness out of the kitchen (see Chapter Nine).

7. Wash your hands before preparing meals and after you go potty (see Chapter Three).

8. Disinfect all drinking water via water filtration, halogenation chemicals or boiling (see Chapter Eight).

9. Properly choose, pack and prepare food, and properly dispose of all leftover food (see Chapter Six).

10. Properly dispose of all human wastes (see Chapters Four & Five).

11. Properly dispose of all litter (see Chapter Seven).

12. Practice safe sex.

13. Keep all your vaccinations up to date.

Figure 2-1
Keep All Your Vaccinations Up To Date

Rub-A-Dub-Dub:
Chapter Three

L end a hand, but not a dirty one. Skin, the outer layer, is an overlapping armor of dead cells that protect the living cells beneath. Under a microscope, this outer layer looks like the surface of the Colorado Plateau from thirty thousand feet: canyons and mesas, cracks and fissures. Resident microbes are wedged firmly into the low spots. Some of these microbes are friendly, serving to keep skin slightly acid and resistant to other microbial lifeforms like fungi. Others, such as S. aureus, are waiting eagerly for the opportunity to cause disease.

Fingers laden with S. aureus and showing hardly a speck of evidence that the digits spent some time exploring the dark passage of a nostril go about the task of chopping onions and adding them to tuna for a sandwich later on the trail. Settled in their new warm and luxuriant home, the microbes grow in leaps and bounds, doubling the population in minutes. In a matter of a few hours a few thousand become hundreds of millions with maximum population reached in about 12 hours. The sandwich may taste okay, but even if a small part is consumed illness will appear four to eight hours later.

Figure 3-1
Bacterial Growth Phases on a Warm Tuna Sandwich

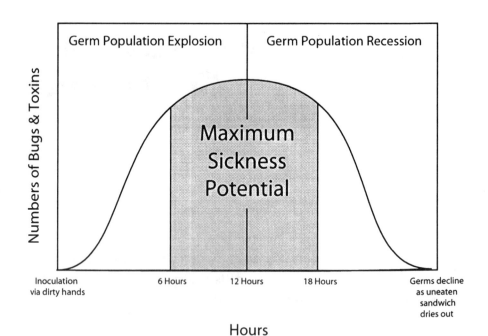

In addition to the residents, transient germs come and go as fortune dictates. They can accumulate rapidly after cleaning up from a bowel movement, and they congregate most thickly under fingernails and in the deeper fissures of fingertips. That's why human hands account for 25 percent to 40 percent of all food-borne illness.

Hand washing prior to food handling or attending to wound care, even with detergents, does not remove all the bacterial flora residing on hands, but it does significantly reduce the chance of contamination.

For your information, science recommends the following eight-step hand washing technique for maximum cleanliness:

1. Wet hands with hot flowing water (100-120°F).

2. Soap up until a good lather is attained.

3. Work the lather all over the surface of the hand concentrating on fingernails and tips. Thirty seconds to one minute of active scrubbing is recommended.

4. Clean under fingernails.

5. Rinse thoroughly with hot water (very important!).

6. Re-soap and re-lather.

7. Re-rinse.

8. Dry (very important!)

This eight-step process, although a lot of extra work in a busy schedule, is based on research observations and years of experience in the health care and food industries. The "very important" emphasis given to two of the steps deserves a closer look.

Hot water and detergent wash the natural oil and the germs trapped within the oil off your hands. Water that is too cool will merely shift the oil around and re-deposit the grime somewhere else on your hands. The same thing occurs when you wash greasy dishes: they remain greasy no matter how much soap and cold water is used. If you want the bugs off your hands, you've got to get the oil off, too.

Drying rates as "very important" because washing alone leaves some bacteria suspended in those last few drops of water. By drying your hands completely, meaning no droplets or freely mobile water remains, you take away the chance that germs will flow into dinner or somewhere else even less desirable. Save a bandanna exclusively for drying your hands after a good washing. Or carry a small absorbent towel. Commercial products that pack easy and absorb wonderfully are available in many outdoor stores (e.g., Camp Towel, 22x28, super absorbent, comes in a resealable plastic bag for easy carrying—see Appendix B).

For most of us hot water is a rare wilderness commodity. But you can still get clean hands with this modified backcountry technique which substitutes germicidal soap for hot water. In tests, adequate hand sanitation was achieved with as little as one-half-liter of water.

1. Wet hands thoroughly.

2. Add a small amount of germicidal soap (Betadine Scrub or Hibiclens or Klenz-Gel Blu will work well).

3. Work lather up, especially fingertips, for 30 seconds to one minute.

4. Clean under fingernails (and keep your nails trimmed).

5. Rinse thoroughly.

6. Repeat soap, lather and rinse.

7. Dry.

Figure 3-2
The Modern Backcountry Kitchen Tool

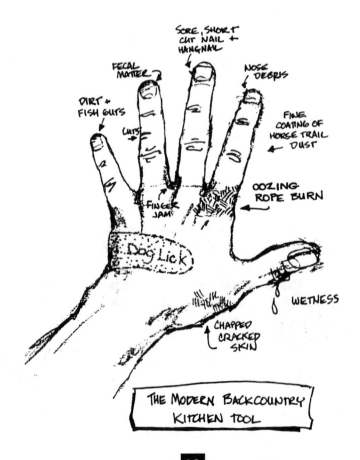

The purpose of the germicide is to kill the transient bacteria where they lie since the small volume of water used is not very effective in removing the nasty organisms. The process of repeating the soap and lather is important since the first lather-up removes the soils that tend to interfere with the work of the germicide letting the second lather be more effective in zapping the microscopic denizens. Sure, it's a bother ... but so is getting sick. And, remember, even plain old unscientific hand washing beats no hand washing at all.

For more information on how germicides work take a peek at Appendix A: Sanitizers and How They Work.

A Note of Caution: Some products advertised for quick hand sanitization, especially in the prehospital emergency care world, are basically pure rubbing alcohol or made with rather potent chemicals that are very harsh to your skin. While these products are appropriate for incidental use, regular use may actually degrade the quality of your skin and promote the growth of undesirable lifeforms. Studies have shown that regular use of some of the no-water instant hand sanitizers increases the number of bacteria on your hands.

The Rest Of The Story

Germs and filth that collect on the rest of your body on a wilderness trip don't typically create a problem ... unless it's social. Oils, in fact, secreted by your skin form a protective layer that helps prevent drying and harm from wind and sun. An exception concerns genitals, especially in women who may be more prone to vaginal infections if their genitals are not cleaned regularly.

Body washing is most easily accomplished by a plunge into a lake or stream with vigorous rubbing of water over your body. In many frigid wilderness water sources, the vigorous rubbing also helps prevent tissue death from freezing.

If you use soap, don't jump in the water. Even "biodegradable" soaps take a long time to biodegrade, and fish are well known to prefer water to soap. Carry pots of water or water in collapsible containers well away from water sources, at least 200 feet, where you can safely soap up and rinse off. In chilly weather, heating a pot of water first allows you to have a rather pleasant experience.

When the sun shines brightly, many people choose to bathe under solar showers, and several commercial products are available in many outdoor stores.

For soaps, there are several healthy choices including Mountain Suds, Campsuds, Dr. Bronner's and Sunshower Soap which suds-up well in hot or cold water. At least one type of soap is available in just about every outdoor store.

Camp Soap, in three "flavors" (pine, citronella and peppermint), even works well in saltwater, comes in liquid concentrate or in a bar with handy travel case and, like most "outdoor soaps," can be used for dishes and clothes too (see Appendix B).

Then there's the unique alcohol-free No-Rinse products. No-Rinse Body Bath requires a little water to suds up but, as the name says, no rinsing. No-Rinse Shampoo is used straight from the bottle followed by drying with a towel or absorbent cloth. There's even a No-Rinse Hair Conditioner (see Appendix B).

For a hot or cold wash, a commercial product, the backcountry Bath Towel, 18x36, alcohol-free and somewhat heavy, comes pre-moistened and sealed in a heatable foil package (see Appendix B).

Figure 3-3
Move At Least 200 Feet From Water Sources to Bathe

Poo-Poo Plans: Chapter Four

S hit, by any other name, smells the same, and you can't realistically pack out everything you pack in, except in special circumstances (such as dragging frozen feces off of winter trips). But you can, with an adequate poo-poo plan, reduce the risk of fecal contamination (to yourself and the environment) to an absolute minimum.

Transmission of fecal-borne pathogens occurs in four ways: direct contact with the feces, indirect contact with hands that have directly contacted the feces, contact with insects that have contacted the feces, and drinking bad water. Human waste products break down to a harmless state as a result of two mechanisms: (1) bacterial action in the presence of oxygen, moisture and warmth, and (2) sterilization over time from direct ultraviolet radiation. Deposition of solid body wastes should include placement (1) to maximize decomposition, (2) to minimize the chance of something or someone finding it, and (3) to minimize the chance of water contamination. And, after the deed, wash your hands.

Latrines are out, except in established spots. They concentrate too much poop in one place. They carry a high risk of water pollution. They invite insect and mammal investigation. They are unsightly, and they stink. If you are ever required to dig a latrine, make it at least a foot deep, add soil after each deposit, and fill it in when the total excreta lies several inches below the surface.

For years, environment- and health-concerned wildland managers have recommended "catholes" as the best thing to do with your doo-doo. Preferably in a level spot, a cathole should be dug several inches into an organic layer of soil, where decomposing microorganisms live most abundantly. After you've dropped your droppings, stir them into the soil to speed decomposition. Cover the mess with a couple of inches of soil, slightly compact the soil and disguise the spot to hide it from later passersby.

It was long assumed that microorganisms in near-surface soil rapidly rendered fecal matter harmless. But then came the turd-testers, scientists who purposefully catholed pathogen-impregnated excrement and dug it up a year after to discover some of the pathogens were still active. And don't assume that the cathole is going to trap the bad bacteria and viruses in the hole forever. Since some of those pathogens can survive for many, many months, and since in those intervening months rain may fall, remember that where the water goes the germs go as well. In tight heavy clay soils, even in wet boggy soils, most bacteria will not migrate far. Sandy soils tell a different story. Viable bacteria can move with ground water for 50 to 100 feet. Viruses like the Norwalk flu may be mobile for 1,000 feet or more.

For these reasons, choose a poo-poo place with attention to soil type (heavy soil is better), climate (dry climates move the germs less), water table (the closer the table to the surface the greater the chance of water contamination) and slope inclination (flat areas are better), and place your poop at least, 200 feet from a water source.

In situations where the soil is sandy and water lies everywhere, catholes, especially when a large group is involved, pose a high risk of environmental contamination. The risk is not insurmountable. The answer is cathole disinfection. Dry and liquid sanitizers, sanitizers that will themselves break down harmlessly, added to the contents of the cathole and stirred carefully, will reduce billions of nasty bugs to a lifeless mass. Your choice of sanitizers is important.

Some of them are hazardous to you and the environment (see Appendix A: Sanitizers and How They Work).

Now it's generally considered that your Number Two will decompose to harmlessness quickest if you use the "smear technique," smearing or scattering your dung over the surface to maximize sun and air exposure. Smears, too, should be at least 200 feet, or approximately seventy adult paces, from water, and placed where little chance of discovery exists.

The smear technique has obvious drawbacks in well-used areas where, for one thing, waste won't decompose fast enough to eliminate health hazards. In those places it remains best to defecate in thoughtfully situated catholes.

Sanitation Around The Nation

Wilderness areas, despite the Wilderness Act of 1964, are not created equal. Some are especially wet, some dry, some cold, and some hot. Special sanitation considerations may be required in special environments.

LAKES AND RIVERS

Moving well away from bodies of water and carefully selecting your poopsite will eliminate most of the health risks associated with water contamination. But in some places, such as deep steep dry-country canyons and island-studded lakes, moving well away isn't possible. In those spots, the only safe alternative is packing it out. The most acceptable means to do this requires a sturdy sealable can and several heavy-duty garbage bags. Line the can, such as a large ammo box, with a couple of garbage bags folded out over the rim. Here is the infamous "groover," so named for the warm red grooves left in your butt after even only a few moments of contemplative pooping. Before and after each use, throw in some chemicals to reduce the smell and slow decomposition (see Appendix A: Sanitizers and How They Work). Note: Rapid decomposition inside a plastic bag may produce a thoroughly disgusting explosion. Toilet paper goes into the bag, too, but urine should be squirted elsewhere. Urine dilutes the added chemicals and greatly increases bag weight. Before packing the bag for the next day's travel, squeeze your nose shut and squeeze out the air and tie the bag firmly closed.

Another option is a commercial product called the Drop-Box, a disposable camping toilet of collapsible cardboard that supports up to 275 pounds. Poop drops into a strong plastic bag which can be easily transported to a waste facility (see Appendix B).

DESERTS

Human excrement won't decompose when it's deeply buried in sandy, predominantly inorganic desert soil. For this reason, deposits should be made far from water sources, out of gullies and other obvious drainages, and off of slick rock. Insect contamination in dry regions is low, and smearing your personal manure rates as a healthier alternative than deeply burying it. Because it will remain visible for a long time, discretion is the better part of desert evacuations, and the best all-round choice in most heavily-trafficked areas is shallow burial. High near-surface temperatures will cook pathogens to death in short order.

SEASHORES

Catholed fecal matter usually decomposes rapidly in moist seashore environments. In less frequented areas, intertidal zones offer the quickest decomposition. Bacteria that encourages decomposition may be one thousand times more abundant there than in sandy areas above the high tide mark. Where visitors are few and tidepools are absent, depositing your dump directly into the sea is probably OK. Before making a seadump, be sure you aren't contaminating beds of shellfish. (Note: Fecal bacteria from municipal sewage spills do often contaminate oceans and beaches.)

When your route of travel takes you well away from shore, fecal matter may be saved in easily-degraded paper bags and thrown overboard when you're in deep water. No definitive tests have been run on sea bottom decomposition of human wastes, but it is well known that fecal bacteria do not thrive in sea water and will slowly die off … good news since seals and sea-going birds are doing it out there all the time. Thoughtful consideration should be given to offshore defecation. SCUBA divers, for example, are likely to be offended.

It's apparently harmless to pee in the sea (see Chapter Five).

ABOVE TIMBERLINE

In the frozen north and in the fragile oft-frozen high country, decomposition goes slowly due foremost to the cold. Fecal monuments may stand for ages. The smear technique offers the fastest decomposition of human wastes, and sun can decontaminate and rain and snow can wash away the smear. Once again, please choose a secluded spot well away from obvious water sources and drainages.

SNOW

Snow-covered stools, no matter how far they're buried, will appear on the surface come springtime. For that reason, proper choice of burial sites remains of paramount importance.

Figure 4-1
Careful Camping Protects Wilderness Water

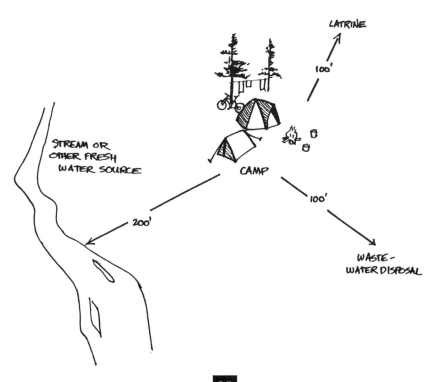

Figure 5-1
Urinate on Rocks to Help Protect the Environment

Urine Trouble: Chapter Five

Although urine is usually considered a sterile waste product, whizzing wherever you please is seldom the best idea. Consider: (1) Pee, in some instances, may draw wildlife that can defoliate plants and dig up soil. (2) Urine can carry, almost always in developing countries, unhealthy parasites such as schistosomes that will be spread by careless urination. (3) Your urine is rich in a compound called urea, a breakdown product of old proteins. Urea breaks down quickly by environmental microbial action to form ammonia. Ammonia at levels as low as one part per million in water can be lethal to many species of aquatic wildlife. If you pee in small non-flowing water sources you could be a death-dealing instrument of ammonial destruction.

To stay on the safe side, urinate on rocks or in non-vegetated spots a reasonable distance from water sources.

On some wilderness waterways, travelers are encouraged to urinate directly into the water. In some areas, this practice is discouraged. Follow local recommendations.

You will cause no harm if you pee in the sea.

Food For Thought: Chapter Six

Bacteria get to foods in a couple of ways: (1) They start there in the raw or newly processed food. Milk, for example, has a resident population of spoilage bugs that will, even with refrigeration, eventually make curds and whey. Almost all dry cereals have a resident population of bacteria seeds called spores. Spores can remain viable for decades. (2) Bacteria are added to the food during preparation, or they are added by incidental contamination.

Most of the bacteria found in fresh food and cooked food pose a problem only to your appetite. They taste like the subject matter of Chapter Four. Spoilage microbes are a critical part of the rot and decay of the natural world which would be a debris-laden mess without them. Controlling spoilage of food on wilderness trips is, however, a tool not only for preventing some illnesses but also for keeping vittles tasty.

Spoilage bacteria grow at a wide range of temperatures. Milk and meat will spoil even at 38°F. Although most germs with pathos prefer warmer climes, a few bad bugs will grow in your backpack on a cool fall day. The notorious Listeria monocytogenes is one cold-loving germ, but serious illness threatens only those humans who are pregnant or resistance-compromised.

The chance of a dangerous bacterial explosion in food is influenced by three factors: dryness, salt content, sugar content. Dryness, or more specifically the water activity, of a food determines its ability to promote bacterial growth. If moisture is not there, the bugs don't have a chance. If moisture is there with high concentrations of salt or sugar, bacteria once again have little chance because the moisture is tightly held by the salt or sugar and the microbes are unable to get a drink. No water, no growth, no problem. Drying, salting and sugaring foods served our ancestors for many generations that never saw a block of ice, and they'll serve you today on your wilderness venture.

Food Choices

Foods like dried fruit, dry cereals and dried meat tend to resist spoilage and seldom support the growth of bad bugs. On occasion you might find some mold making a stand on food with low water activity, spoiling an old low water activity snack. Salted meats and salted fish may put a substantial decline in the water bottle contents of those humans who consume them, but they tend to resist spoilage due to the tight salt-grasp on the little water that remains. Low-moisture cheeses (dry Monterey Jack, Romano and the like) can be carried safely for many days. It's helpful to keep them cool enough to prevent the butterfat from separating and making a mess. These cheeses are great for adding flavor to bacteria-free dehydrated foods, and they're a source of high calories.

High-moisture foods (e.g., packaged meats, some cheeses) and low-salt spreads are fertile fields for bacteria to romp and stomp. Sometimes high-proteins foods come "pre-inoculated" with bugs of pathos due to errors in quality control where they're manufactured. Any non-dried or non-salt-heavy animal product must be looked upon with a critical eye. After a warm day in your pack, eating any of these foods can be a crap shoot ... so to speak.

Carrying frozen meats on a winter trip is more feasible, yet introduces another concern. For your safety always assume raw meat and poultry are contaminated with some pretty serious bad guys. The National Academy of Science revealed in one study that up to

66 percent of all poultry sampled contained Campylobacter and/or Salmonella. Campylobacter is the real cause of what many people call the 24-hour-flu. Salmonella is much more serious and potentially life-threatening for some folks. The answer: thorough cooking. The interior temperature of burger or bird should reach at least 170°F. Since you probably won't have a meat thermometer, cook the meat until all the red is out and the bugs should be out, too.

Even well-cooked meat may have created a problem: what did the meat touch and what touched the meat on its journey from the package to the fire? If you put the meat in a pan with your hand and then opened a candy bar to stave off hunger while the meat cooked, you can still get sick. If you sliced the meat and then sliced the cheese with the same knife, you can still get sick. Unwashed hands, knives and cutting surfaces have all produced wilderness trip-shortening results.

If you haven't converted to wilderness-oriented vegetarianism by now, you should at least prepare meats with thoughtfulness.

For those who like to explore the shores of the sea, many have learned the Epicurean delights of the animals that live in shells. Some of you have even learned to enjoy these bivalves raw, and most of time there is no regret and little embarrassment from dining on clams, oysters or mussels. A couple of notes may save you more than face. Where humans and their sewage are dumped into the sea, bivalves can concentrate enough bacteria and viruses to make you really ill: E. coli, Shigella, Salmonella, Norwalk virus, Hepatitis A. The solution is cooking. They are still delicious, and cooking takes most of the worry out of a close personal encounter with your favorite mollusk.

There are exceptions. The risk of Paralytic Shellfish Poisoning from bivalves and Demoic Acid Poisoning found in some crabs are not eliminated by cooking. The toxins are heat-resistant and once you show signs of poisoning it's too late to turn back. Ask local humans and follow their advice about consuming local sealife. When in doubt check with local health departments.

Leftovers

Some "shit" hasn't had the opportunity to be processed by the human digestive system. This stuff results from cooking more than you can eat, which is a result, most often, of less than maximum meal planning skills. Storage of cooked-but-uneaten leftovers in the wilderness poses an almost insurmountable problem.

Your safest bet is to not eat leftovers.

Buried food usually ends up being unburied by hungry animals. If campfires are appropriate, small amounts of dry food will burn to nothing, but wet food usually becomes an unsightly lump of ash unless the fire is extremely hot. Scattering small amounts of food in seldom-visited areas does not spoil the harmony of nature (for most humans), and may be considered as a safe disposal method. Leftover food should ideally be sealed in plastic bags and packed out.

Successful anglers face the question of what to do with the "leftover" heads and guts of fish. Scattering fish parts widely in secluded spots probably rates as the best disposal method in most cases. Throwing the fish remains into cold wilderness water is a poor method of disposal since the parts will stay visible for a long time. Where hungry bear populations are dense, water disposal of unused fish parts might still be the best idea. It could prevent parts of you from becoming the leftovers of a bear's meal.

Guidelines for Maximum Safe Food Handling and Preparation

1. Choose processed foods over raw foods for your wilderness trip.
2. Cook food thoroughly.
3. Once food is cooked or rehydrated, consume it.
4. If leftovers must be eaten, reheat the food thoroughly.
5. Wash and sanitize hands prior to food and water preparation (see Chapter Three).
6. Use only safe water for food preparation.
7. Keep individual eating utensils out of community dishes.

8. Do not eat any high-moisture food that has been warm for an hour or more.

9. On group trips, plan and prepare food in groups no larger than two to four people.

10. Do not share prepared food between groups.

11. Provide individual supplies of things like trail mix.

12. Do not share personal utensils, water bottles, etc.

13. Keep anyone with the slightest indications of a cold, flu or skin infection out of the camp kitchen.

The Clean Camp: Chapter Seven

As any sanitation engineer can tell you, much can be learned about a person by going through their personal refuse. Same goes for backcountry trash and, in the plus column, the amount of litter has steadily decreased in wilderness areas over the last twenty years despite an increase in litter bearers, thank you very much. The potential impact of trash (inorganic waste brought into the backcountry as opposed to garbage which is organic) ranks low as a health hazard when compared to, say, the disposition of leftover food and, far more important, human waste products. Still, keeping a clean camp and leaving a clean camp are important considerations in wilderness hygiene.

Start by reducing the amount of your litter at the source. Repackage your wilderness foods into reusable containers. Remove any excess packaging. The less you have to leave behind the less chance you'll leave something behind.

Paper may be burned if building a campfire is feasible, allowed, environmentally safe and ethically acceptable. Be sure you're burning paper. Much of the "paper" packaging today has non-burnable foil or plastic lining.

If you packed in plastic, tin and aluminum cans, tin foil and glass then pack it out. Better yet: pack everything out!

Water Disinfection: Chapter Eight

L ong gone are the days when you could drop your exhausted body to the ground beside a sparkling flow of wilderness water and plunge your face into the cold rush for a drink. Pathogens inhabit, to some degree, most of the world's water. How tragic! And, unless you're willing to risk gut-ripping misery, how important to carry some means of water disinfection on extended wilderness trips.

Water "disinfection," by the way, is the proper term in most cases of wilderness water treatment. Water "purification" means removing impurities that alter taste and color, but it does not necessarily mean pathogens have been removed. Water "sterilization" means all the microorganisms have been removed from the water and not just pathogens.

There are three proven ways to guarantee your backcountry water is safely disinfected:

Boiling

The rule is very simple: once the water is hot enough to produce one rolling bubble, it is free of organisms that will cause illness, worldwide and up to at least 19,000 feet above sea level. The reason:

all of the time it takes to bring water to a boil works toward the death of organisms in the water. By the time water reaches the boiling point it's safe. Giardia lamblia cysts, for instance, die at approximately 122°F. If you want to "feel" safer, let the water roll around at a boil for a couple of minutes. Boiling is cheap (the only cost is fuel) and effective, but it consumes time and it's inconvenient if you run out of water on the trail.

Thermal Death Curve of Virulent E. Coli: A Case in Point

At 140°F, death occurs in 8.34 minutes.

At 145°F, death occurs in 2.11 minutes.

At 150°F, death occurs in 0.53 minutes.

At 155°F, death occurs in 0.13 minutes.

Halogenation

As for chemicals that kill water-borne pathogens, both chlorine and iodine have been proven effective, given enough of the chemical and enough time (see Appendix A: Sanitizers and How They Work). Halogenation is affected by water temperature, the pH of the water and the turbidity of the water. Halogens are generally more convenient and faster than boiling the water (when you consider lighting the stove or building the fire), but they cost more and can't be guaranteed to work as effectively. Halogens also leave the water tasting crummy, a phenomenon reversible by adding flavoring (e.g., energy drink powders) after the disinfection process has been completed. If you flavor the water prior to complete disinfection, the added substances may disrupt the disinfection process.

AQUACURE

AquaCure tablets are a combination of flocculating and coagulating agents (which produce rapid sediment formation) and chlorine (which disinfects the water). Being effervescent, the tablets dissolve quickly, and, after 10 to 20 minutes, a sediment containing entrapped pollutants forms and settles to the bottom of your water bottle. Anything left suspended in the water is killed by the chlorine including bacteria and viruses. The sediment needs to be strained out through any clean material ... a clean T-shirt will work. AquaCure is the only tablet that clarifies as well as disinfects polluted water. In clear water, of course, no sediment forms, but disinfection still takes place. It comes in a box of 30 tablets, individually sealed to maintain potency, that will treat about 33 quarts of water and sells for around eight dollars (see Appendix B).

BLEACH

Household bleach (four to six percent sodium hypochlorite) will kill most pathogens in water. Two "drops" of bleach should be added to one quart of water followed by a 30 minute wait. If the water does not have a slight chlorine odor and taste after 30 minutes, add two more drops and wait 15 more minutes.

HALAZONE

Halazone tablets are chlorine-based water disinfectants. If you buy halazone tablets you must follow the directions on the label, adding the proper number of tablets for the amount of water being disinfected. The wait is usually 30 minutes, and the taste is usually remarkably bad. You don't see halazone as much as you used to.

IODINE

Tincture of iodine (two percent concentration) will disinfect water. Add five "drops" per quart of clear water or 10 "drops" per quart of cloudy water, and wait 30 minutes. The water tastes like iodine. Tincture of iodine is available from most pharmacies.

POLAR PURE

Polar Pure (USP-grade iodine crystals) kills most pathogens when added to water. You add water to the special bottle in which the crystals come, and then add the iodine solution you've created to your drinking water. The bottle tells you how much to use depending on water temperature. A three-ounce bottle will disinfect about 2000 quarts of water for about $12. The water tastes like iodine. Polar Pure is available in most outdoor stores.

POTABLE AQUA

All water-borne pathogens are killed by the iodine in Potable Aqua (globuline-tetraglycine hydroperiodide) if the proper amount and the proper wait are used. One or two tablets are used depending on the clarity of the water. Follow the directions on the label. A bottle of 50 tablets will disinfect 25 to 50 quarts of water for around five dollars. The water tastes like iodine. Potable Aqua is available in most outdoor stores.

SIERRA WATER PURIFIER KIT

Chlorine crystals are used to disinfect the water of all pathogens, and an oxidizing liquid (hydrogen peroxide) is then added to neutralize any free chlorine which removes the bad taste. One kit will usually disinfect 160 gallons of water at a cost of about $15. The kit is available in most outdoor stores.

Filtration

Water filters physically strain out some of the organisms and contaminants in water that could cause disease. Structurally, there are two basic kinds of filters: (1) Surface or membrane filters are thin perforated sheets that block impurities. (2) Depth filters are made of thick and porous materials that trap impurities as the water is forced through. The effectiveness of filters varies greatly from one that removes only relatively large particles such as Giardia lamblia to one that removes virtually everything removable. Viruses are too small to be filtered out, but some filters kill viruses with iodine from resins on the filter as the water passes through. Mechanically, once again, there are two basic types: (1) Pump-feed filters that require manual force to push the water through the filter. (2) Gravity-feed filters that just hang there while water drips via gravity through the system.

Filtered water looks *clean*, but the purity of the water depends on the specific filter. Read the claims of a filter carefully before your purchase. They are available in a wide variety of costs, shapes and sizes. Filtration, in general, costs more but offers the quickest route to safe water.

Figure 8-1
Relative Sizes of Small Things That Make You Sick

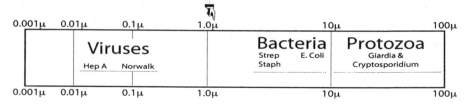

Lower Limit
of Best Water Filters

0.001μ	0.01μ	0.1μ	1.0μ		10μ	100μ
	Viruses			Bacteria	Protozoa	
				Strep E. Coli	Giardia &	
	Hep A	Norwalk		Staph	Cryptosporidium	

0.001μ	0.01μ	0.1μ	1.0μ	10μ	100μ

μ = 1 micron = 1 millionth of a meter

BASIC DESIGNS

Basic Designs is a company giving you a choice of either a couple of gravity-feed filters or a pump-feed filter.

On the gravity-feed side, the best choice is the Pocket Size Ceramic Filter. The filter sits in the bottom of a plastic bag made to hang from tree limb or tent pole. Gravity forces clean water down the outlet hose into your water bottle. It only weighs 12 ounces, but it takes about 40 minutes to fill a one-quart bottle. Physical removal of protozoa and bacteria is complete, and an activated carbon core removes trace elements and bad taste. The filter can be cleaned in the field, and the manufacturer claims up to 1,000 gallons of filtration before the unit has to be replaced. Suggested price is about $70.

On the pump-feed side, the Ceramic Filter Pump has PVC tubing that holds the plastic pump directly to the filter while the filter goes directly into the water. A pre-filter keeps the big stuff out, and the outlet hose, attached to the pump's handle, has a clip to hold it to the lip of your water bottle. One stroke moves one ounce of water, and the filter will last for up to 500 gallons of filtration. Weight is only seven ounces. It should remove everything except viruses and it costs about $30 (see Appendix B).

FIRST NEED

General Ecology has been making water filters for over 10 years. Their line of First Need filters includes the Deluxe Water Purifier, a practical option for the wilderness adventurer. The single-action pump sucks water up 14 inches of sturdy tubing, pushes it through a separate filtering canister, and out six inches of discharge hose into your water bottle. If you opt for the pre-filter (an excellent idea) and cap, you've got eight parts connected at six places, and it may take both hands and both feet to operate the system. The whole thing weighs about one pound and packs with relative ease. It pumps out about one pint of water per minute, and the manufacturer claims you can get up to 800 pints before the filter has to be replaced. Pumping requires little effort.

In the sealed canister hides the filter matrix of carbon and proprietary materials, providing safe water in three ways: (1) A depth filter physically traps protozoa and bacteria inside the canister. (2) The electrostatically charged surface of the filter holds onto any debris with the opposite charge. And (3) the carbon adsorbs (causes molecules to stick to its surface) pesticides, herbicides, solvents, even odors and bad tastes such as iodine and chlorine.

On the downside, the ability of carbon to adsorb has a threshold, and once the particular threshold of a substance is reached, the filter will let that particular material through. But the filter will still let water through so you can't tell that it's no longer adsorbing.

Like all filters, the First Need Deluxe will eventually clog and have to be replaced. You can put off the inevitable by periodically attaching the pump to the filter's outlet and "backwashing" with clean water. Before storage, a flush with a dilute chlorine solution (dilute household bleach will work) further extends the life of the filter by killing off germs or fungi that might be left clinging. The pre-filter, which screens out anything 10 microns or larger, increases the filter's life expectancy even more.

You can usually find the Deluxe for approximately $40, the replacement filter for $25, and the pre-filter for $10 (see Appendix B).

KATADYN

Long before backcountry filtration systems began to proliferate, Katadyn was there. They've been there for nearly 50 years. Like all finely crafted Swiss products, Katadyn filters are dependable, durable and precisely manufactured. They have the look and feel of a fine tool.

The Katadyn Pocket Filter has a double-action pump (pumps water with pushes and pulls on the handle) that brings water up 28 inches of strong supple hose and forces it through a ceramic filter. A metal strainer at the inlet keeps large debris out of the hose. Clean water squirts out a small spout at the top of the pump which means you have to aim the flow into your water bottle, a sometimes awkward procedure. The unit weighs in at a solid pound-and-a-half, but packs very neatly into a carrying case. It produces about one quart of water for every 90 seconds of pumping. Pumping requires effort. The silver-impregnated ceramic filter mechanically and efficiently strains out protozoa and bacteria. The silver creates a bacteriostatic condition … bacteria, fungi, even algae won't grow on the filter … which means cleaning is simplified. When flow through the filter slows, clean the filter with the supplied brush, and normal function should return. When cleaning, keep in mind you may be scrubbing off a considerable amount of accumulated contaminants. Beware of disposing of these contaminants inappropriately, and clean your hands afterwards. Dry the filter before storing, and it may outlast you. Silver does not increase the effectiveness of the disinfection system, and the Katadyn does not remove chemical pollutants, bad tastes or offensive odors. Cost is around $250.

The Katadyn Mini Filter has the same filter ceramic element as the Pocket Filter, but it lies only seven inches long and weighs in at eight ounces. It can be cleaned about 100 times yielding around 1,000 gallons of water in its life time. The cost is about $150 (see Appendix B).

MOUNTAIN SAFETY RESEARCH (MSR)

MSR entered the water filter market only a few years ago, but the company has a long history of high-quality, innovative gear … and the WaterWorks is no exception. The pump is a strong plastic cylinder with a lever-type handle. The long inlet tube includes a float and a weighted strainer, so the end of the tube hangs near the surface of the lake or stream, out of the debris on the bottom. On the outlet end, you can put a tube into your water bottle or screw the whole pumping unit onto a standard water bottle. Floating inlet, long pumping handle, and convenient outlet make the WaterWorks easy for one person to use. It fills a one-quart bottle in less than a minute. Unit weight is about 18 ounces, and it comes with a handy carrying case.

MSR utilizes a four-part filtering system, each filter with progressively smaller pores, beginning with a foam sponge in the strainer, continuing to a10-micron stainless steel filter, on to a carbon filter, and ending with a 0.1 micron membrane. All bacteria, protozoa and particulate matter stays out of your drinking water. On the downside, the sponge on the strainer ends clogs very easily if there is silt or sand suspended in the water. And periodically, the stainless steel filter needs to be scrubbed, the carbon filter needs to scraped clean with a knife, and the membrane has to be replaced when it clogs. (Note: The manufacturer recommends replacing the carbon filter after the third scraping. And, as with all carbon filters, it has an adsorption threshold.) Also on the downside, the MSR has several small parts that eventually wear out and need replacing including an O-ring and a check valve. The company recommends a dilute bleach flush and drying before storing. The cost is around $140 for the unit, $30 for the membrane, $20 for the carbon filter, and $12 for the maintenance kit (see Appendix B).

PUR

Recovery Engineering's PUR Explorer is innovative and remarkable. A 130-micron strainer on the inlet tube keeps the big chunks out of the pump. (Note: It will still clog if it falls into deep muck on the bottom.) The pump's size (almost 12 inches long) and its large handle make it easy to hold and use. A curved hook-like end on the outlet tube allows you to fill any water bottle quickly, if you don't get too excited pumping. And it's fast. Unit weight is a hefty 21 ounces with carrying case.

A glass-fiber filter removes protozoa and small sediment, but the real secret is contained in the tri-iodine-impregnated resin matrix. Contact with the resin kills bacteria and viruses making the Explorer an excellent choice for around-the-world travel. The iodine, bonded to the resin, adds a little taste to the water the first few times you use the filter, but it goes away after a few gallons have been pumped through. If you just can't stand the taste of iodine at all, an add-on carbon filter is available for an add-on cost of about $20.

On the downside, since you can't taste the iodine, you don't know when its effectiveness has worn off. But the manufacturer says the filter element will fail long before the iodine supply is used up.

More ingenuity involves the Explorer's self-cleaning mechanism. When the pump starts to clog, water squirts out a relief-valve on the handle to warn you. Simply twist the handle a quarter-turn and pump a few more times, and a built-in brush scrubs the filter without the pump being taken apart. (Note: Water squirting out the special valve on the handle is not clean.) No special preparations prior to storage are required. Cost runs around $130.

The PUR Scout has the same purification system that eliminates the danger from protozoa, bacteria and viruses. It weighs 12 ounces and lies nine inches long. It does not self-clean and when it clogs the filter has to be replaced for about $35. It clogs quickly in silty water. The initial cost of the unit is about $65.

The PUR Hiker removes protozoa and most bacteria, weighs 11 ounces, lies 7.5 inches long, handles easily and costs about $45. Most of your money pays for the filter ($35) which must be replaced when it clogs. For most of the world this is a great water filter (see Appendix B).

SWEETWATER

SweetWater, Inc., makes the Guardian, the newest and most attractive water filter on the market. It's attractive primarily because (1) the double-action lever works fast (you can fill a one-quart bottle in less than a minute) and with the greatest ease of any filter, (2) it can be cleaned quickly and simply in the field with the enclosed brush, and (3) it costs only about $50. The depth filter removes protozoa and bacteria, and with the additional ViralGuard cartridge (for an additional $20) you will also be guaranteed that no active viruses enter your water bottle. The Guardian, with the cartridge attached, provides safe water worldwide.

Activated charcoal in the depth filter removes pollutants and bad tastes. A pre-filter floats in water and keeps the big stuff out of the system. You can get an adapter that fits snugly inside the lip of your water bottle to hold the outlet tube securely in place. It'll pump approximately 200 gallons before the filter needs to be replaced (for about $20). For about $65 you get a water filter that does everything except pump itself.

The Guardian weighs eight ounces and packs into a carrying case at less than eight inches by four inches (see Appendix B).

TIMBERLINE

On the lightweight and convenient side of pump-feed filters, it's hard to beat the Timberline. Its plastic pump attaches directly to the separate filter which goes directly in the water source. Unit weight is only six ounces, and if that's too much you can leave the pump at home and use the additional plastic tube as a straw to suck water right up from the stream through the filter. This system is very easy to use, and you can pump, or suck, one quart in around 90 seconds.

Timberline Filters mechanically strain out all protozoa, but bacteria and viruses will flow freely through this system. In many areas where you travel protozoal removal will be enough, but, if you're unsure about the presence of bacteria, the use of the Timberline cannot be recommended. And the filter clogs easily when the water source contains sediment and debris. Pre-filtering, with something such as a coffee filter, will eliminate the clogging problem. The manufacturers recommend a vinegar flush and thorough drying before storage. Cost is under $30 (see Appendix B).

PENTAPURE

Water is poured through PentaPure's patented penta-iodide resin which has been proven to have 1,000 times the killing power of the older tri-iodide resin. No pumping. It's a gravity-feed system. NASA has been using penta-iodide to guarantee astronauts safe water.

Most convenient for hikers and paddlers is the PentaPure Travel Cup. Its four ounces are barely noticeable. Simply place the purifier unit, like a funnel, over the mouth of your water bottle, and pour in the water. It's on the slow side, requiring about two-and-a-half minutes to fill a one-quart bottle. Since the resin does not block the passage of things like protozoa, the manufacturers recommend a wait of three minutes more to ensure everything harmful in the water is entirely dead.

For longer trips and larger groups, PentaPure makes a collapsible Water Jug (1.25 pounds empty) that holds two gallons: same resin, same microscopically pure water.

The Cup ($30) or the Jug ($44) will purify 100 gallons of water, but there's no way to know if the resin is used up unless you've kept track of how much water you've poured through it which is very inconvenient (see Appendix B).

Figure 8-2
Disinfect All Wilderness Water Before Drinking

Keeping A Klean Kitchen: Chapter Nine

A clean wilderness kitchen starts before you pack the car and head for the trailhead. Kitchen gear, including your pocket knife, need to be cleaned prior to packing. How many times has backcountry pot come out of the pack and, oops, a germ garden plot is already well established. The type of gear you choose—aluminum, stainless steel, wood—is irrelevant as long as you keep it clean.

Set your kitchen up at least 200 feet from any water sources, and choose a spot that will be minimally impacted by the kneeling, sitting and walking around you'll be doing during the food preparation process. Sand and rocks make good kitchen areas. Heavy duff or even heavy mature vegetation return quickly to their natural state. Sparse vegetation and fragile young vegetation may be marred for years to come by one night of cooking. If you have to move logs or rocks to make your kitchen comfy, put what you disturbed back where you found it before moving on.

Too many cooks spoil the broth and the environment. If you're part of a large group, break up into smaller cooking groups of no more than four people. Your small kitchen group should include no one with indications of colds or flu (no matter how slight), with obviously injured hands or with dirty hands (which means those hands need to be washed even if they look clean).

Dirty dishes will be their cleanest if they're washed with water suitable for drinking. The best kitchen clean-up water has been brought to or almost to the point of boiling. Soaps, especially soaps sold for backcountry use (the "environmentally safe" soaps), tend to have less ability to remove fats and proteins. To make the soap work best you need hot water. Water at 120°F (it's almost too hot to keep your hand in it) will work fine. Water at 80°F will start redepositing soluble waste back on the bowls and spoons. If you clean as much of the visible stuff out of your cooking pot as possible, put it into eating bowls and put a pot of water back on the stove or fire right away, cleaning water will be ready by the time you finish consuming your wilderness repast.

To maximize camp hygiene your kitchen gear should be rinsed in water disinfected with a sanitizer (see below). Disposal of your rinse water then poses another potential environmental hazard. Ideally, your waste water should go into its own "cathole," 100 feet from camp, 200 feet from any water source and well above the ground water table. A couple of inches of natural debris (leaves, needles, twigs, etc.) in the bottom of the hole will further help to trap waste until it is deactivated.

Kitchen Klean-Up By The Numbers

1. Remove as much of the visible waste as possible.

2. Wash the kitchen gear in hot soapy water using an abrasive pad to scrub everything well.

3. Rinse the gear well using either clean hot water or water disinfected with an acceptable sanitizer. Iodophors or chlorine work well at a level of 50 to 200 parts per million (ppm). Disinfected water needs to sit for 10 minutes after you've added the sanitizer (see Appendix A: Sanitizers and How They Work). Let the washed gear soak in the rinse water for a couple of minutes.

4. Dry the cleaned gear as much as possible.

Note: On cold weather trips where the temperature stays below 38°F your gear will remain relatively low in germs if you allow it to cool off rapidly, and if you bring your next meal to the boiling point during preparation.

Sharing Is Not Always Caring

Nice people are willing to share, but they may be passing around more than their water bottle. Personal eating and drinking gear should stay personal. And the same rule should apply to your lip balm and your toothbrush. If you can't finish your candy bar or your lunch, dispose of the leftovers properly instead of passing your germs to someone else.

Wilderness food usually shows up in plastic bags and food contamination can be further reduced by pouring the food out instead of reaching in for it. When you pack for your trip, prepare a separate bag of snack foods (e.g., trail mix) for each individual.

Figure 9-1
Proper Waste Water Disposal

The Healthy Zoo: Chapter Ten

It's a jungle out there ... or, more accurately, it's a "zoo." A healthy camp needs to take into account the fact that you're going to be neighbors, at least most of time, with wild animals which means you should be considering zoonoses. Zoonoses does not refer to the proboscises of wild animals but to zoonotic diseases, those diseases that can be passed from an animal other than a human to a human. This type of disease transmission involves moving germs from one animal to another. The transmission of a microbe from a wild animal to a human can occur in several ways.

1. Direct transmission is just that, and the classic example is rabies. The rabies virus is spread via the infected animal's bite. It has the virus in its saliva, the saliva is laid in the wound, and the virus begins its trek toward the victim's brain along nervous tissue cells.

2. Indirect transmission can occur in two ways: via an insect messenger such as a tick that bears Lyme disease or Rocky Mountain spotted fever, or via the consumption of contaminated meat such as eating undercooked bear meat and getting the disease trichinosis.

You, as an outdoorsperson, do not rank high as an opportunity for most zoonoses ... unless you're a hunter or, for some other reason, you find yourself handling wild animal blood, guts, secretions and excretions ... but the incidence of several animal diseases in wild populations, including rabies and plague, are on the rise. Your most excellent chance of getting sick, remember, is from the germs you pack into the wilderness.

Hantavirus Infection

Hantavirus, the rodent-carried respiratory disease, has shown up in at least 16 states now. All of the patients have had fever and muscle aches, and most have had at least one of a group of other symptoms including cough, headache and abdominal pain. Sounds like any old sickness, but the hantavirus also causes an acute onset of difficulty breathing which has led to death for a number of humans.

The virus is in the rodent's urine and, possibly, the saliva and feces. The virus can become air-borne through misting of the urine or dust from feces or rodent (primarily mice) nests. You breathe in the virus, you get sick. You also might be able to swallow the virus. So far it appears as if the virus is not transmitted from one human to another. If you suspect you have contacted the hantavirus you should seek medical attention immediately.

To reduce the chance of hantavirus infection, do not camp near rodent nests or burrows. Sleep in a tent or on a ground cloth that extends at least two feet beyond your sleeping bag. Keep your camp clean so rodents are not attracted.

Leptospirosis

Although infected wildlife shows no signs of the disease, animals shed the Leptospira organisms freely in urine. Human cases, usually less than 100 each year in the United States, are often acquired from contact with contaminated water and, sometimes, soil. You can also get sick from infected animal blood and tissues. Swallowing ranks as the primary way Leptospira get inside humans, but the organisms can "worm" in through abraded skin and through the mucous membranes of eye and mouth. Leptospirosis appears throughout tropical and temperate regions of the world, and is most commonly seen in Southeast Asia and some areas of Latin America. Recent cases have been brought back from lower Central America.

Numerous types of Leptospira exist, but the signs and symptoms they produce in humans are much the same. One to two weeks (can be as long as three) after becoming host to the spirochetes, the first of two phases of the disease begins. Phase one lasts 4-7 days and shows up in many patients as fever, chills, headache, enlarged lymph nodes, malaise and a nonproductive cough. After a couple of days off, the disease reappears in a second phase with a lower fever and a severe headache that won't go away. A "spotty" rash sometimes appears. Muscle aches, stomach pain, nausea and vomiting can result in either or both phases. Death occurs about five percent of the time, most often in the very young and very old. Outdoorspeople who play in rivers (e.g., kayakers) in high risk areas are especially likely to become infected. Find a doctor as soon as possible.

Plague

Carried by rodents and passed primarily by the bite of rodent fleas, both rodent and flea are killed by the organisms, an unusual aspect of this disease. Black rats are especially susceptible. In the United States deer mice and various voles maintain the bacteria. It is amplified in prairie dogs and ground squirrels. Other suspects include chipmunks, marmots, wood rats, rabbits and hares. States in which plague still exists include New Mexico, Arizona, California, Colorado, Utah, Oregon and Nevada.

Hikers and campers in infected areas are at risk. Meat-eating pets that eat infected rodents (or get bitten by infected fleas) can acquire plague. Dogs don't get very sick, but cats do. There is only one known case of plague being passed to a human by a dog, but cats can pass the disease to humans by biting them, coughing on them, or carrying their fleas to them. In the wild, coyotes and bobcats are known to have transmitted plague to humans after the critters were dead and the humans were skinning them. Skunks, raccoons and badgers are suspect. Sick people transmit plague readily to other people.

Several forms of plague exist, but the common signs are fever, chills, malaise, muscle aches and headaches. Blackened bleeding skin sores appear with one form. Gastrointestinal pain with nausea, vomiting and diarrhea is common.

If plague is suspected, it should be treated. Fatalities are common. Find a doctor as soon as possible. Prevention includes avoidance of rodents, avoiding touching sick or dead animals, and restraining dogs and cats while traveling in infected areas.

Rabies

Wild hallucinations including episodes of unexplainable terror, extremely painful difficulty swallowing to the point of refusing all liquids and drooling constantly ("hydrophobia"), frequent muscle spasms especially in the face and neck, and, toward the end, complete disorientation and a raging fever: rabies.

Since rabies causes no reaction until it reaches the central nervous system, you don't know you're infected until it's too late to save you. Once replication of the virus starts in the brain, nasty deaths have invariably resulted.

Of the multi-thousands of humans that die annually, only a few are in the United States ... 18 documented cases since 1980. And 10 of those acquired the virus on trips to foreign lands. Over the past 20 years, the number of cases of rabies in domestic animals has steadily dropped, due primarily to animal vaccination programs. Often thought of as a disease of carnivores, any mammal can theoretically have rabies, and cows are the most common domestic animal to carry the disease. Despite the publicity mad dogs have received, rabid cats outnumber rabid dogs, with 290 infected cats being destroyed last year, and 182 infected dogs. But the last two decades have shown a steady increase in the number of wild animals having the virus.

Just because you get bit, doesn't mean you'll get sick. Not every animal that has rabies transmits it. On the high end of estimates, 80 percent of the rabid animals that might bite you will give you the disease. The others don't have enough of the virus in their saliva. Skunks tend to be especially dangerous, secreting more of the virus over a longer period of time, and hanging on tenaciously when they do bite. Of course, smelly considerations keep most humans out of skunk bite range. Raccoons, conversely, tend to appear cute, cuddly and approachable, but they can be very deadly. Rodents, such as woodchucks, die of rabies, but rarely if ever secrete the virus in their saliva.

Just because you don't get bit, doesn't mean you won't get sick. Infection can occur when saliva contacts open wounds or mucosal membranes (such as your nose and mouth). The lick of a dying dog could kill you. Humans have gotten rabies from breathing the virus in bat-ridden caves where tons of bat saliva and excretions collect.

If you are bitten by a rabid animal, your life expectancy depends on where the teeth sank in. In rare cases, it has taken a year for the virus to reach an infected human's central nervous system. Usually it takes about 60 days for the virus to reach your brain after a bite on the lower leg, but only about 20 days from a bite on the face. Hands fall in between. So a bite on the nose should send you looking for a doctor faster than a bite on the toe.

Early symptoms of rabies are too general to cause concern: fatigue, headache, irritability, depression, nausea, fever, stomach pain. Sounds like another day at the office. There is only one way to know for sure if you have the disease. Unfortunately the proof results in your death. There are ways to guess you have the virus ambling around inside you, in which case you will want to get the shots that kill the germs before they reach your brain.

Ways To Guess You Have Rabies

1. The incidence of rabies in the species that bit you. Domestic dogs and cats, ferrets, mice and rabbits, for instance, are low risk. Raccoons and skunks are high risk.

2. The behavior of the animal that bit you. Most wild animals intelligently run away from humans. An unprovoked attack might mean rabies. A raccoon, skunk, fox or bat wandering around in full daylight shows abnormal and suspect behavior. Foaming at the mouth shows up in about half the cases. To confuse things,

some animals have dumb paralytic rabies, carrying the virus while appearing restless and sick, instead of the snarling, slobbering Cujo form of the disease called furious rabies.

3. The vaccination status of the animal that bit you. Vaccination of domestic animals does not guarantee protection, but it lowers the risk.

4. Your vaccination status. People who work with animals often get a pre-exposure immunization. It is highly effective, but requires a booster soon after the bite. Failure to be boosted can be fatal.

Ways To Keep From Dying Of Rabies

1. Appropriate and immediate care of the wound rates as extremely important. Rabies virus dies quickly when exposed to sunlight, UV radiation, dry air, heat and detergents. Bites from suspect animals should be washed aggressively as soon as possible with soap and water.

2. If the biting animal can be safely captured or killed and taken, head intact, to the nearest public health department, it can be either watched for signs of rabies or tested for rabies. Testing requires some of the animal's brain tissue ... which requires the killing of live animals. Without conclusive lab tests, bites from wild raccoons, skunks, bats, coyotes, bobcats, and other carnivores should be considered rabid, and you should get the shots that prevent rabies from developing.

Tick-Borne Diseases

Only mosquitoes, worldwide, transmit disease more often to humans than ticks. In the United States ticks are more guilty.

A number of measures lessen the likelihood of acquiring a tick or a tick-borne illness. Do not camp in places where you know ticks are running rampant. Clothing should be light colored so that ticks can better be seen on them. Long-sleeved shirts and long pants should be worn, trousers should be tucked inside a pair of high socks. Contact with brush should be avoided if possible. A permethrin tick repellent should be applied to clothing prior to exposure, with particular attention to the ends of shirt sleeves, pants, and about the collar area. A repellent containing DEET (a concentration no greater than 35% is recommended) may be applied to the skin in the same areas, but overuse should be avoided, especially in children. A full body inspection for ticks should be performed daily.

Ticks may not attach themselves for several hours after initial skin contact, and, in this state, can be easily removed. Once they have attached themselves, which is usually painless to you, detachment is substantially more difficult. Since transmission of infection is frequently delayed following tick attachment, attached ticks should be removed immediately when discovered. (If possible the tick should be preserved in rubbing alcohol for later identification.)

No simple, effective method of causing the tick to detach itself is known. The best method of tick removal is to gently grasp the animal with tweezers as close as possible to the point of attachment, and remove by applying gentle traction. It is advisable, though not always possible, to remove the mouth parts with the rest of the tick. A small piece of skin may come off painlessly with the tick, which means tick removal is almost always complete. Every effort should be made to avoid crushing the tick and contaminating either patient or helper with crushed tick material. The wound should then be cleansed with soap and water, and a Band-Aid applied. Tweezers should be disinfected after use.

1. Lyme Disease: Lyme disease is a recently recognized, widespread, tick-borne inflammatory illness. In the U.S., areas of high risk are the Northeast, the upper Midwest, California, southern Oregon, and western Nevada. Most cases develop between May 1st and November 30th. The first abnormality is almost always an expanding well-defined red rash. Flu-like symptoms often develop shortly after the rash appears.

Months after the initial infection, if untreated, arthritis may develop, usually affecting the knees and shoulders. Persistent and varied neurologic abnormalities may occur and persist for years.

Medications shorten the duration of Lyme disease and often prevent later problems. Consult your physician.

2. Rocky Mountain Spotted Fever: In many areas of the U. S., especially Montana, Oklahoma, Missouri and the Carolinas, ticks can transmit the germs causing Rocky Mountain spotted fever, an illness characterized initially by fever, headache, sensitivity to bright light, and muscle aches. On the third to fourth day of fever, a pink rash usually appears. If not treated promptly with antibiotics the disease may be lethal. Individuals with these findings, with known or suspected tick contact, should obtain professional assistance as soon as possible.

3. Relapsing Fever: Relapsing fever is an acute febrile illness caused by Borrelia spirochetes. Infected ticks, previously attached to wild rodents, are the prime vectors for this disease. Clinically, initial symptoms are those of an acute flu-like illness, but bouts continue at weekly intervals. The diagnosis is established by identification of the organism in blood smears. Antibiotics knock the bugs down. Prophylactically, one should avoid staying in rodent infested areas, especially in old abandoned cabins.

4. Colorado Tick Fever: This disease is an acute benign viral infection that occurs throughout the Rocky Mountain area during spring and summer. It is characterized by fever, muscle aches and headache. There is no specific therapy.

5. Tick Paralysis: Tick paralysis begins with leg weakness. An ascending flaccid paralysis follows, which progressively worsens as long as the tick is attached to the patient (usually a child). Speech dysfunction and difficulty swallowing are late signs, and death from aspiration or respiratory paralysis may occur. Removal of the tick results in a progressive return to normal neurologic function. Both diagnostically and therapeutically, early meticulous examination for imbedded ticks is mandatory.

Trichinosis

Encysted in skeletal muscle, the larvae of the parasitic worm Trichinella spiralis are eaten. In the small intestine, the worms mature and mate within a few days, usually within 48 hours. Female worms deposit larvae in nearby mucosal tissue. Larvae enter the circulatory system of the animal and invade skeletal muscle. Within three weeks, the larvae are encysted and ready to be infectiously passed should anything eat the muscle of the animal that ate the muscle of the animal that had encysted larvae.

Although all carnivorous or omnivorous mammals may have trichinosis, consumption of raw or undercooked pork accounts for the vast majority of the disease in humans. Rodents are often infected, but mice and rats seldom grace a human palate. Bears, raccoons, opossums, seals, walruses, peccaries and wild swine are common hosts, and sometimes are eaten by humans.

Trichinosis produces gastrointestinal symptoms during the first week after ingestion of infected meat: pain, nausea, vomiting, variable diarrhea. During the second week, as the larvae migrate around your body, capillary damage occurs, commonly producing facial swelling. Migrating larvae can invade the pulmonary system, causing a cough and chest pain, or the heart muscle, causing a chance at patient death. Gastrointestinal symptoms may remain for 4-6 weeks, until the worms are all excreted. As the larvae encyst in muscle tissue, significant muscle aches and stiffness often result. Between six and 18 months after ingestion, the larvae die and become calcified. This period is usually asymptomatic.

No drug exists for safe and effective treatment. Supportive treatment is indicated until the disease has its way with you. Cooking meat until it reaches at least 150°F kills the parasite. Most Trichinella larvae are also killed by freezing if meat is frozen long enough. Holding meat at minus 20°F for 6-12 days ends the life of the larvae. Warmer freezing temperatures require longer freezer time.

Tularemia

Since 1967 less than 200 cases per year have been diagnosed in the United States. Though certainly once a disease associated with unhealthy contact with rabbits, ticks are now, by far, considered the prime transmission mode for the bacteria. Although many species of ticks have been incriminated, dog ticks and lone star ticks rank as the most common reservoirs. Since the infecting organisms have not been found in tick saliva, it is thought they are carried in tick feces. Rabbits still qualify as the second most common vector, but you must handle infected tissue, as you might do by skinning and eviscerating the little bunny. (Wearing rubber gloves will prevent transmission.) You could pick the disease up in water or soil, too, by direct contact, ingestion or breathing in contaminated dust or water particles.

About 80 percent of tularemia cases appear as red bumps that harden and ulcerate, usually on the lower extremities where ticks bit, or on the hands from handling infected tissues. Ulcers are typically painful and tender. Enlarged tender lymph nodes are common. The second most common form of tularemia, the typhoidal form, causes fever, chills and debility. Weight loss may be significant. Lymph node enlargement is less. Pneumonia is a relatively common complication of tularemia.

Treatment of choice is drugs. Contact a physician.

The Good Neighbor Camping Plan
1. Be selective about your choice of campsites. Avoid obvious animal nests, burrows and other places they bed down. Avoid places with obvious feces and obvious animal pathways especially paths leading to water.
2. Sleep in a tent or on a large groundcloth which keeps ticks away, dust off your face unless the wind is blowing and other unwanted critters out of your bed.
3. Keep all food in tightly sealed containers and off the ground to prevent attracting the "little people" into camp.
4. Disinfect all drinking water.
5. Keep your kitchen gear clean.
6. Wash your hands regularly and thoroughly.

Appendix A:
Sanitizers & How They Work:

Chemicals that have the ability to inactivate or kill germs quickly make life a whole lot safer. Consider the epidemics of typhoid fever and cholera that ravage lesser developed countries today. The bacteria that cause these diseases and many more are readily destroyed by a host of relatively inexpensive and comparatively safe-to-use compounds. Knowing how these chemicals do what they do may help you decide which to use under what circumstances.

One basic concept that seems to get lost in the debate over which compound is best concerns the relationship of "concentration" and "time." Any chemical that significantly reduces great numbers of germs has to either be in contact with the bugs in enough concentration or for enough time. So for any chemical that does an effective job, be it chlorine in water or some antibiotic in you, the effectiveness falls along a continuum between a very high concentration for a very short exposure and a very low concentration for a very long exposure.

One factor that determines which chemical to use is a simple matter of toxicity. If the sanitizer (or drug) kills the germs and the host, somebody messed up. When sanitizers are used on human skin the concentrations of the chemical are usually low but use is for a long time. Recommendations for hand washing that suggest a 30-second scrub (instead of a quick rinse) and prescriptions that tell you to swallow an antibiotic once a day for two weeks (instead of all at one time) take this principle into account. There's no point in burning down the barn to get rid of a couple of mice. Use a dose that works and no more.

A Case In Point

Let's say you have used a stainless steel cooking pot to soak an infected finger. Now it's dinner time, macaroni will be the next thing in the pot and it's getting dark. You are carrying Clorox bleach (5% hypochlorite solution). To disinfect the pot you can add a little bleach to water in the pot and swish it around for a long time, or add lots of bleach and swish it a short time. Both will work equally well in terms of killing germs.

Other considerations include your supply of Clorox, the "hurry" factor and the quality of the surface of the pot. An old rusted oily pot is harder to sanitize than a new slick steel surface.

You need to also consider where you will pour out a strong concentration of the bleach. The "killer tea" you've brewed will go on killing for some time after you discard it. Thoughtful disposal is necessary.

Understanding how chemicals sanitize requires a little imagination. Germs are microscopic critters with a cellular anatomy and physiology similar to yours. The machinery of their cell, as with your many cells, is based on proteins and the complex chemistry of protein enzymes. Enzymes are the directive chemists of the cell. Should sensitive cell anatomy or the enzymes of the cell be disrupted, the cell may die, or at least lose its ability to reproduce. Sanitizers, in general, are chemical cell disrupters.

Sanitizers can be classed in several categories. The various types have advantages and disadvantages that may help you decide which will be appropriate for various wilderness applications.

Halogens

Chemicals such as chlorine, iodine, bromine, fluorine and ozone are great and greedy oxidizers. Oxidation substantially changes whatever is oxidized. Rust, the result of oxidation, significantly alters a shiny new piece of steel. Halogens alter the vital organs and enzymes of microbes. They "rust" germs to death.

Chlorine has the advantages of being very inexpensive and very effective for sanitation over a short period of time at 100 to 200 parts per million (ppm). Its disadvantage is that it works best on clean surfaces or in clean water. Debris reacts with chlorine leaving little to hunt out and zap the bacteria. A healthy "zap," by the way, is a 90 percent reduction in the number of bugs.

Chlorine, until fairly recently, had to be carried in liquid form, especially dangerous if the container leaked. A new stabilized dry chlorine compound in tablet form is now available. This chlorine complex is more effective in a soiled environment since the chlorine is released from the carrier compound of the tablet on demand. The commercial brand of these tablets is Effersan (see Appendix B). One-fourth tablet in one gallon of relatively clear surface water yields approximately 150 ppm. In backcountry applications as a final rinse for dishes and hands, you can sanitize with confidence. Other applications of this convenient tablet include the disinfection of catholes and rendering shitcans sanitary and much less offensive.

Chlorine in the backcountry, on the negative side, will go on reacting with the stuff of nature after you pour it out. It adversely affects wild animals and must be kept out of all natural water sources. Chlorine solutions should be poured in a hole well away from water when discarded.

Iodine is the other halogen most commonly used. Iodine in its simple form and in "tamed" forms (such as iodophors) makes a great sanitizer. Tamed iodines have been the skin sanitizers of choice in hospitals for decades. For your hands, pots, pans and for water disinfection it works equally well as long as a sufficient concentration is used for a sufficient amount of time. Approximately 25 to 75 ppm will achieve the same kill power as chlorine at 150 ppm.

(Note: Iodine loses its effectiveness in alkaline water that might be found in parts of the Southwest.)

Iodine costs more than chlorine, and it stains. It does not appear to create the same environmental hazard. Pouring an iodine solution over a rock surface or spreading it over a dry dirt area may be an alternative to pouring it in a hole.

A Huge Note of Caution: Never ever mix substances that contain halogens. For example, if you mix iodophor, which contains phosphoric acid, with chlorine, a potentially deadly chlorine gas may be released.

Catholes and Groovers: A Case In Point

The chemical of choice for disinfecting catholes and groovers is one of the halogens in a strong solution (500 to 1,000 ppm) stirred carefully into the most recent deposit. Dry powdered swimming pool-type chlorines or rehydrated Effersan tablets will kill bacteria. Caution must be taken to avoid contact with your eyes and skin. It is just like handling household bleach.

Other dry compounds that could be carried on river trips include either calcium hydroxide (slack lime) or calcium oxide (quick lime). Both are quite caustic and kill by raising the pH of the contents of the groover. Great care must be taken to keep dry limes dry. Once wet they create a large amount of heat and can literally take the hair off your hide (one of its past uses by hide tanners).

Quatenary Ammonium Compounds

Quats are cationic detergents unique in that they contain no halogens yet are good skin and hard surface sanitizers. They kill germs by altering some important cell structures and proteins. Quats were developed long ago and are used to a lesser extent today.

Acid Anionic Detergents

LDBSA and DDBSA are names too big and unwieldy to even write, but they are detergents active against a wide range of bacteria. They appear to work by punching holes in the cell wall of the germ which, like most living things with big holes punched in it, goes on to die.

These detergents will sanitize hands and kitchen gear without the environmental concerns of halogens. Being slightly acidic they tend to dry out your skin. The product Klenz-Gel Blu should be considered as a new addition to your germicidal arsenal (see Appendix B).

Chlorhexidine Gluconate

CHG is another detergent-like germicidal compound widely used for hand and hard surface sanitation. It works by messing up the machinery of the germ cell. Look for the brand name Hibitane in a variety of products sold for personal and kitchen use. It has an added benefit of leaving a bacteriostatic rinse film when used at concentrations of at least 150 ppm.

Hot Water

Heat, although not a chemical, does to microbial protein what a hot frying pan does to an egg. The resulting proteinous glump can no longer perform its germy function. When using hot water the same rules of concentration and time apply, but in this case concentration equals temperature. A spoon, say, immersed in boiling water momentarily will be disinfected. If you boil water in a pot, the interior of the pot is disinfected. A five-minute soak in water at 170°F will do the same job.

Appendix B: Resources

THE LIFE AND TIMES OF GERMS: CHAPTER TWO
Benenson, Abram S., *Control of Communicable Diseases in Man, Fifteenth Edition*, American Public Health Association, 1015 Fifteenth Street NW, Washington, DC 20005.

RUB-A-DUB-DUB: CHAPTER THREE
Adventure Foods, Route 2 Box 276, Whittier, NC 28789; (704) 497-4113 (Camp Towel and excellent soaps).

Black River Enterprise, P. O. Box 129, Apache Junction, AZ 85217; (602) 844-8009 (Bath Towel).

N/R Laboratories, Inc., 900 East Franklin Street, Centerville, OH 45459; (800) 223-9348. (No-Rinse Body Bath, No-Rinse Shampoo, No-Rinse Hair Conditioner).

Sawyer Products, P.O. Box 188, Safety Harbor, FL 34695; (800) 940-4464 (Camp Soap).

POO-POO PLANS: CHAPTER FOUR
Hampton, Bruce, and David Cole, *Soft Paths: How to Enjoy the Wilderness Without Harming It*, Stackpole Books, P. O. Box 1831, Harrisburg, PA 17105.

Black River Enterprise, P. O. Box 129, Apache Junction, AZ 85217; (602) 844-8009 (Drop-Box).

THE CLEAN CAMP: CHAPTER SEVEN

Hodgson, Michael, *The Basic Essentials of Minimizing Impact*, ICS BOOKS, Inc., 1370 East 86th Place, Merrillville, IN 46410. (800) 541-7323.

National Leave No Trace Program, Information and Materials, 288 Main Street, Lander, WY 82520; (800) 332-4100.

WATER DISINFECTION: CHAPTER EIGHT

Basic Designs, Inc., P. O. Box 2507, Santa Rosa, CA 95405; (707) 575-1220 (Ceramic Pump, Pocket Size Ceramic).

General Ecology, 151 Sheree Blvd., Exton, PA 19341; (215) 363-7900, or place orders at (800) 441-8166 (First Need).

Katadyn USA, Inc., 3020 N. Scottsdale Road, Scottsdale, AZ 85251; (800) 950-0808 (Pocket Filter, Mini Filter).

Mountain Safety Research (MSR), P. O. Box 24547, Seattle, WA 98124; (206) 624-7048 or (800) 877-9677 (WaterWorks).

Recovery Engineering, 2229 Edgewood Avenue South, Minneapolis, MN 55426; (612) 541-1313 or (800) 845-PURE (PUR Explorer, Scout and Hiker).

Safesport Manufacturing Company, P.O. Box 11811, Denver, CO 80211 (AquaCure).

SweetWater, Inc., 2505 Trade Center Avenue, Longmont, CO 80503; (800) 557-9338 (Guardian).

Timberline Filters, P. O. Box 3435, Boulder, CO 80307; (303) 494-5996. (Timberline Filter).

WTC Industries, Inc., 14405 21st Avenue North, Minneapolis, MN 55447; (612) 473-1625 or (800) 637-1244 (PentaPure).

THE HEALTHY ZOO: CHAPTER TEN

Tilton, Buck, and Frank Hubbell, D.O., *Medicine for the Backcountry, Second Edition*, ICS BOOKS, Inc., 1370 East 86th Place, Merrillville, IN 46410; (800) 541-7323

Forgey, William W., M.D., *Wilderness Medicine, Fourth Edition*, ICS BOOKS, Inc., 1370 East 86th Place, Merrillville, IN 46410; (800) 541-7323.

APPENDIX A: SANITIZERS AND HOW THEY WORK

Effercept Products Division, Micrel Ltd., Inc, P. O. Box 1248, Laramie, WY 82070; (800) 841-0410 (Effersan).

Ecolab, Inc., 840 Sibley Memorial Highway, Mendota Heights, MN 55118; (612) 451-5600 (Klenz-Gel Blu).

Index

Try These Other Books By
Buck Tilton

- Backcountry First Aid and Extended Care 2nd. Edition
- B. E. of Rescue from the Backcountry
- Cooking the One Burner Way
- Medicine for the Backcountry 2nd. Edition
- Ozone, UV And Your Health
- Sex in the Outdoors